WHAT ARE KEYSTONE SPECIES?

SEA STARS

A MARINE KEYSTONE SPECIES

KATHLEEN A. KLATTE

PowerKiDS press

Published in 2025 by The Rosen Publishing Group, Inc.
2544 Clinton Street, Buffalo, NY 14224

First Edition

Editor: Theresa Emminizer
Book Design: Tanya Dellaccio Keeney

Photo Credits: Cover Sergey Skleznev/Shutterstock.com; p. 5 blueeyes/Shutterstock.com; p. 7 LifeisticAC/Shutterstock.com; p. 9 Nuagesucre/Shutterstock.com; p. 11 PT Hamilton/Shutterstock.com; p. 13 Marina Poushkina/Shutterstock.com; p. 15 Daniela Calota Lita/Shutterstock.com; p. 17 volkann/Shutterstock.com; p. 19 Greg Amptman/Shutterstock.com; p. 21 Vitoriano Junior/Shutterstock.com.

Cataloging-in-Publication Data

Names: Klatte, Kathleen A.
Title: Sea stars: a marine keystone species / Kathleen A. Klatte.
Description: Buffalo, NY : PowerKids Press, 2025. | Series: What are keystone species? | Includes glossary and index.
Identifiers: ISBN 9781499446685 (pbk.) | ISBN 9781499446692 (library bound) | ISBN 9781499446708 (ebook)
Subjects: LCSH: Starfishes–Juvenile literature. | Marine ecology–Juvenile literature. | Keystone species–Juvenile literature.
Classification: LCC QL384.A8 K525 2025 | DDC 593.9'3–dc23

Manufactured in the United States of America

CPSIA Compliance Information: Batch #CSPK25. For further information contact Rosen Publishing at 1-800-237-9932.

CONTENTS

SPECIAL SEA STARS

A sea star is a special marine, or ocean, animal. Sea stars are a keystone species. That means they're a species, or kind, of animal that's very important to the place in which they live.

Though they might not look like it, sea stars are predators! They prey on mussels and other animals in their marine homes. Without sea stars, there would be too many mussels. Mussels would crowd out other animals and cause harm. Sea stars are important because they help make biodiversity possible.

IN FACT!

BIODIVERSITY IS WHEN LOTS OF DIFFERENT PLANTS AND ANIMALS LIVE IN THE SAME PLACE.

AT LOW TIDE, SEA STARS CAN BE SEEN ON THE SHORE.

NOT A FISH

People like to call sea stars "starfish," but they're not fish. They're invertebrates, meaning they don't have a backbone. Instead of walking or swimming, they creep across the ocean floor.

Sea stars mostly eat animals that live in shells, like clams and mussels. They use their arms to pull the shell apart. Some kinds of sea stars use their arms to move food into their mouths. Others push their stomach outside their body to swallow their food.

IN FACT!

MOST KINDS OF SEA STARS HAVE FIVE ARMS. SOME CAN HAVE AS MANY AS 24 OR EVEN 50! IF A SEA STAR LOSES AN ARM, IT CAN USUALLY GROW ANOTHER TO TAKE ITS PLACE.

SEA STARS HAVE HUNDREDS OF THESE LITTLE TUBES UNDERNEATH THEIR BODIES. MOST KINDS OF SEA STARS ALSO HAVE A SUCKER AT THE END OF EACH ARM.

SO MANY SEA STARS

There are thousands of species of sea stars. They are found in all the oceans of the world. Many different kinds live in the Pacific Ocean. Sea stars reproduce by laying eggs. Some can have more than 2 million eggs at a time.

That's not the only way sea stars **reproduce**. If a sea star is cut into pieces, sometimes the pieces can grow into whole new sea stars! Fishermen learned this when they tried to kill sea stars.

THIS SEA STAR WILL PROBABLY REGROW ITS LEGS. THE MISSING LEGS MIGHT EVEN GROW INTO ONE OR TWO NEW SEA STARS.

A SEA STAR'S HABITAT

Sea stars live in habitats, or natural homes, called tidal pools. Tidal pools are shallow, or low, pools of seawater that form on rocky parts of seashores.

Tides are the regular rising and falling of sea levels at the shore. During low tide, the water flows out of the tidal pool. Birds come to eat the sea creatures that are uncovered. During high tide, the water rises again. The fresh seawater contains lots of **plankton**, which many tidal pool animals eat.

IN FACT!

MANY OF THE ANIMALS THAT LIVE IN TIDAL POOLS HANG ONTO ROCKS. THIS HELPS THEM STAY PUT WHILE THE WATER FLOWS IN AND OUT OF THE POOL.

DURING LOW TIDE, MANY DIFFERENT ANIMALS CAN BE SEEN IN TIDAL POOLS.

ADAPTATIONS

Animals that live in tidal pools have special adaptations. An adaptation is a change in an animal that helps it live better in its environment, or natural surroundings.

Snails and mussels close their shells so they don't dry out at low tide. Limpets, barnacles, and sea stars stick themselves to rocks so waves don't wash them away. Sea urchins have spines so other animals won't eat them. Anemones have **tentacles** that help them catch things they want to eat.

IN FACT!

CRABS AND BARNACLES LIVE IN TIDAL POOLS. THEY BELONG TO A GROUP OF ANIMALS CALLED CRUSTACEANS. CRUSTACEANS HAVE A HARD COVERING CALLED AN EXOSKELETON OUTSIDE THEIR BODY INSTEAD OF BONES INSIDE.

ALTHOUGH THESE SEA ANEMONES LOOK LIKE PLANTS, THEY'RE REALLY ANIMALS!

TOO MANY MUSSELS!

Mussels are a kind of sea creature called bivalves. This means their body is covered by a shell made of two pieces. Clams and oysters are also bivalves.

Mussels are **filter** feeders. They have special body parts called gills, which they use to get **oxygen** from the water. Their gills also filter plankton from the water. This is how they eat. Mussels reproduce by laying eggs. A single mussel can release millions of eggs each year. Only about 5 percent of the eggs grow up, but that's still a lot of mussels!

THERE ARE NO SEA STARS IN THIS PICTURE. THERE ARE LOTS OF MUSSELS, BUT ONLY ONE SEA URCHIN AND NO ANEMONES, SPONGES, OR LIMPETS.

IN FACT!

BIVALVES ARE PART OF A LARGER GROUP OF ANIMALS CALLED MOLLUSKS. MOLLUSKS HAVE SOFT BODIES AND NO BACKBONE. MOST OF THEM HAVE HARD SHELLS.

AN IMPORTANT EXPERIMENT

A scientist named Dr. Robert Paine thought of the idea of keystone species. Sea stars helped him to understand it!

In the 1960s, Paine did an important **experiment**. He took all the sea stars from a tidal pool. He moved them out to sea so they wouldn't die.

Paine studied the pool for a year. Without sea stars to eat the mussels, the mussels crowded out many other kinds of animals. Another pool with sea stars still had lots of different animals.

IN FACT!

LIKE SEA STARS, MANY OTHER KINDS OF KEYSTONE SPECIES ARE PREDATORS. WITHOUT THEM, THERE'S NOT ENOUGH FOOD AND SPACE FOR EVERYTHING THAT LIVES IN THEIR HABITAT.

DR. PAINE'S WORK HELPED PEOPLE UNDERSTAND THE IMPORTANCE OF KEEPING KEYSTONE SPECIES SAFE.

SEA STARS IN DANGER

One of the biggest dangers to sea stars is a disease, or sickness, called sea star wasting syndrome (SSWS). The disease can kill a sea star in just a few days. Many kinds of sea stars can get the disease. So many sunflower sea stars have died from it that they could become endangered, or at risk of dying out completely.

Scientists think the disease is linked to global warming. Global warming makes the oceans warmer. It also changes the water so it's not as healthy for the plants and animals that live there.

IN FACT!

GLOBAL WARMING IS THE RISING OF EARTH'S TEMPERATURE. HUMAN ACTIVITIES AND POLLUTION CONTRIBUTE, OR ADD TO, GLOBAL WARMING.

THE GREENHOUSE EFFECT HAPPENS WHEN HEAT FROM THE SUN IS TRAPPED INSIDE THE EARTH'S **ATMOSPHERE**. THIS WARMS THE PLANET.

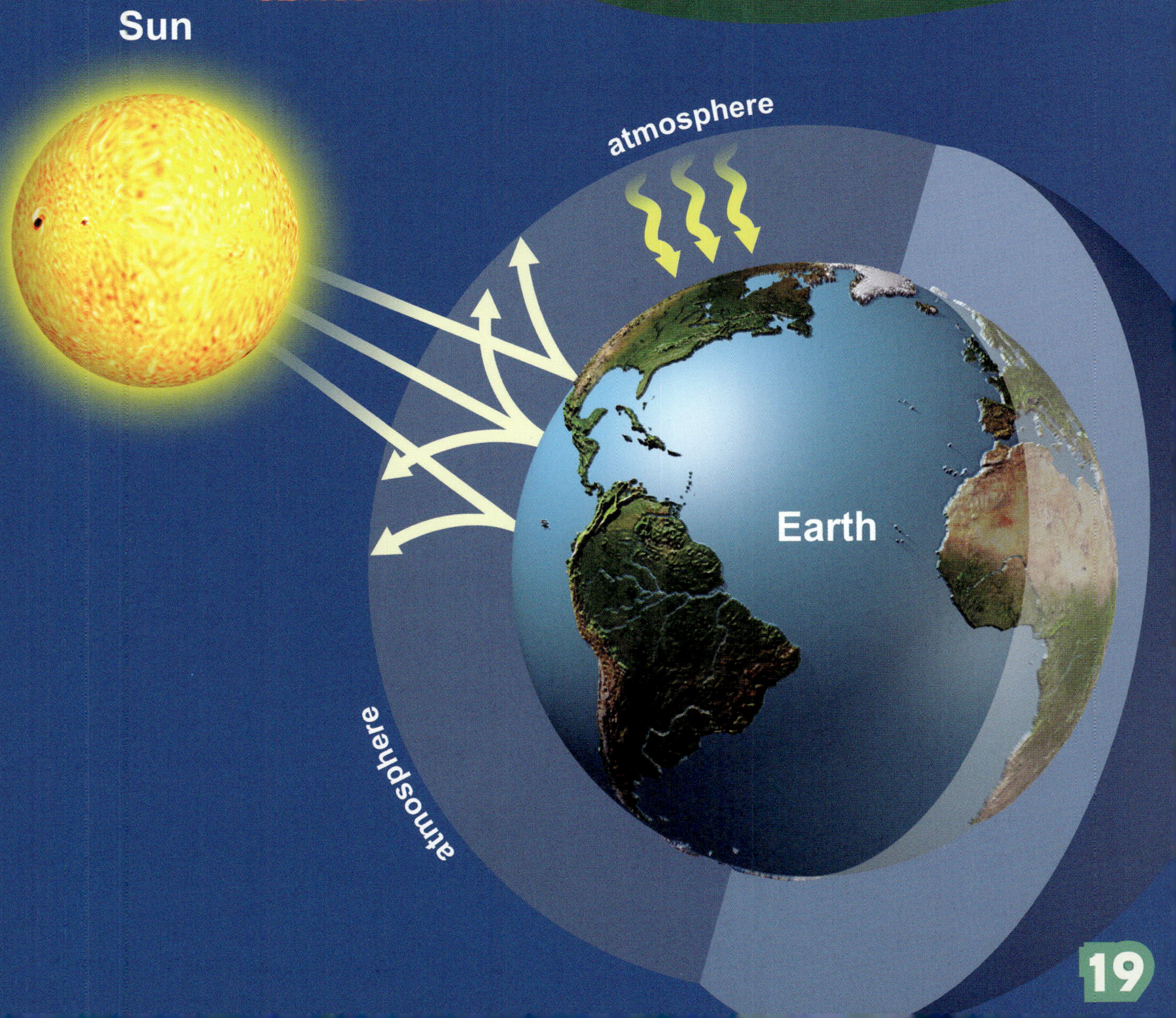

HOW CAN YOU HELP?

One of the best ways to help sea stars is to reduce, or cut down, the amount of trash you make. When we throw things away, they often end up in the ocean where they can cause harm. This is especially true of plastic. Simply choosing to use a glass or metal water bottle instead of a plastic one is a great way to reduce pollution!

The small choices we make every day matter. You can help keep sea stars safe.

IN FACT!

PLASTIC NEVER REALLY GOES AWAY. IT BREAKS DOWN INTO TINY PIECES IN THE OCEAN. THOSE PIECES MIX WITH PLANKTON. IT CAN MAKE THE ANIMALS THAT EAT IT SICK.

THESE KIDS ARE KEEPING THE OCEAN CLEAN BY PICKING UP TRASH ON THE BEACH.

GLOSSARY

atmosphere: The mass of air that surrounds Earth or another planet.

experiment: A scientific test in which you perform a series of actions and carefully observe their effects in order to learn about something.

filter: To pass through something to remove unwanted material.

oxygen: A colorless, odorless gas that many animals, including people, need to breathe.

plankton: A tiny plant or animal that floats in the ocean.

pollution: The act of water or land becoming unsafe for people or animals.

reproduce: To produce babies, young animals, new plants, etc.

temperature: How hot or cold something is.

tentacles: One of the long, flexible arms of an animal (such as an octopus) that are used for grabbing things and moving.

FOR MORE INFORMATION

BOOKS

Sexton, Colleen A. *Sea Stars.* Minnetonka, MN: Kaleidoscope Publishing, 2023

Zimmerman, Adeline. *Sea Stars.* Minneapolis, MN: Pogo Books/Jump!, 2022.

WEBSITES

National Geographic Kids

kids.nationalgeographic.com/animals/invertebrates/facts/sea-star

Read more interesting information about sea stars!

Ocean Conservancy

oceanconservancy.org/blog/2019/01/03/7-facts-sea-stars-world/

Find out more about what makes sea stars so special.

Publisher's note to educators and parents: Our editors have carefully reviewed these websites to ensure that they are suitable for students. Many websites change frequently, however, and we cannot guarantee that a site's future contents will continue to meet our high standards of quality and educational value. Be advised that students should be closely supervised whenever they access the internet.

INDEX